Duke Ellington's
Nutcracker Suite

Anna Harwell Celenza ❋ *Illustrated by* Don Tate

🌉 Charlesbridge

To my husband, Chris . . . beyond category in every way
—A. H. C.

For my beloved uncle, Iowa Blues Hall of Fame's
Harlan Thomas, who creates magic with his music
and cuts the meanest high-top fade
—D. T.

Published by Charlesbridge
85 Main Street
Watertown, MA 02472
(617) 926-0329
www.charlesbridge.com

Library of Congress Cataloging-in-Publication Data
Celenza, Anna Harwell.
    Duke Ellington's nutcracker suite / Anna Harwell Celenza ; illustrated by
Don Tate.
        p. cm.
    Summary: Tells the story of how jazz composer and musician Duke Ellington,
along with Billy Strayhorn, created his jazz composition based on Tchaikovsky's
famous Nutcracker Suite ballet.
    ISBN 978-1-57091-700-4 (reinforced for library use)
1. Ellington, Duke, 1899–1974—Juvenile fiction. 2. Strayhorn, Billy—Juvenile
fiction. 3. Tchaikovsky, Peter Ilich, 1840–1893. Shchelkunchik—Juvenile fiction.
[1. Ellington, Duke, 1899–1974—Fiction. 2. Strayhorn, Billy—Fiction. 3. Jazz—
Fiction. 4. Musicians—Fiction. 5. African Americans—Fiction. 6. Tchaikovsky,
Peter Ilich, 1840–1893. Nutcracker suite—Fiction.] I. Tate, Don, ill. II. Title.
PZ7.C314Du 2011
[E]—dc22   2010023060

Printed in Singapore
(hc) 10 9 8 7 6 5 4 3 2 1

Illustrations done in India ink, acrylic watercolor, and chalk on 140-lb.
    Fabriano Artistico watercolor paper
Display type set in Bodega Serif and P22 Cruz Brush and text type set in Adobe Caslon
Color separations by KHL Chroma Graphics, Singapore
Printed and bound July 2011 by Imago in Singapore
Production supervision by Brian G. Walker
Designed by Diane M. Earley

Las Vegas, Nevada.

In 1960 Las Vegas was the land of opportunity—a new frontier in the world of entertainment. All the stars were there: Frank Sinatra, Sammy Davis Jr., Dean Martin, and more. Perhaps the brightest star of all was Duke Ellington, an American pianist, composer, and big-band leader.

In early 1960 Duke Ellington and his band were the featured act at the Riviera Hotel. Night after night they played to sold-out audiences. Duke's best friend, Billy Strayhorn, helped him compose the music. Their dance tunes were all the rage.

Record producers from across America flocked to Vegas to talk with Duke, but only Irving Townsend said what the bandleader wanted to hear.

"You're the boss, Duke. Record whatever you want," said Irving. "Just give me the go-ahead, and I'll draw up a contract."

"Well, Strays, what do you think?" Duke asked. "Should we make a deal?"

"Depends," said Billy. "What do you want to play?"

"I want to challenge myself . . . create music that can't be categorized," answered Duke. "Got any ideas?"

Billy looked out at the twinkling lights of the slot machines. A cold breeze wafted out of the air conditioner. Someone hit a jackpot. The sound of tinkling coins reminded Billy of sleigh bells. "What about Tchaikovsky's *Nutcracker Suite*?" he asked.

Irving stared at him without saying a word.

"Everybody loves the *Nutcracker*," said Billy.
"Isn't that Christmas music?" asked Irving.
"Of course!" replied Billy. "Tchaikovsky's *Nutcracker* ballet is the new holiday tradition. Haven't you seen it on TV? Who can resist the Sugar Plum Fairy and the Nutcracker Prince? The dancing reed pipes, the waltzing flowers—it's mesmerizing!
"Duke, we have to do it," Billy continued excitedly. "You couldn't ask for better dance music."

Irving shook his head. "I don't know," he said, turning to Duke. "Think about this long and hard. Your listeners want jazz, not classical ballet."

Duke leaned forward slowly. A smile spread across his face. "My listeners want *me*," he said, "and I won't let them down. I think Strays is onto something." Duke elbowed Billy and chuckled. "The boys will squawk when they hear about this. We're going to have fun!"

He turned to Irving. "If you want me to sign, it's the *Nutcracker* or nothing."

The record contract was drawn up. Studio space was reserved, and Duke and Billy went to work. They studied Tchaikovsky's score and listened to recordings of the ballet. Nothing got in the way of their plans—not even hectic travel schedules. Duke went to California to work on a film score. Billy went home to New York. But every night they discussed the *Nutcracker* over long-distance telephone calls.

"We have to update the music for modern listeners," said Billy. "Tchaikovsky used an orchestra with violins and cellos. We need to make the most of our saxophones and brass."

"And don't forget our cats on bass and drums," said Duke. "They'll keep the pulse of our *Nutcracker* jumpin'."

Duke and Billy worked as a team, seamlessly blending their musical ideas. As they traveled from city to city, their composition grew into a timeless musical map. A little Vegas glitz appeared here and there, but that wasn't the only place to leave its mark. Los Angeles, New York, and New Orleans were there, too. Hollywood glamour mixed with the Harlem Renaissance as each dance tune fell into place. By the end of May, the new *Nutcracker Suite* was ready to be recorded.

The band arrived at Irving's Los Angeles studio early in the morning. Billy waited for Duke before starting rehearsal. He knew the musicians were going to complain, and he didn't want to face them alone.

A half hour passed before Duke strolled in. He was always late.

Billy passed out the music. "Here's our latest masterpiece," he said. "Let's start with the overture."

"Overture? What kind of snooty title is that?" asked Ray, a trumpet player.

Booty put down his trombone. "We came here to play jazz," he said. "I don't do ballet."

"We came here to play *music*," said Duke. "Now listen to Strays."

"Cats, this isn't the *Nutcracker* you're used to," said Billy. "Duke and I changed the mood a bit. All the themes are there, but they're wearing different threads—get it?"

Booty moaned. Ray rolled his eyes. Billy pretended not to notice. He turned to the bass player and snapped his fingers. "Okay, Aaron, let's take that bass for a walk. A-one, a-two, a-one-two-three-four."

Aaron played a deep, bluesy bass line. Sam, the drummer, picked up the pulse. Saxophones and brass joined in, and the studio became a glittering ballroom. Paul played a sax solo. Booty followed with his trombone and plunger. The highlight was supposed to be the trumpet melody, but Ray wasn't cooperating. "Put some heart into it!" Duke exclaimed. "Show the ladies how that horn of yours can dance!"

The next piece was based on Tchaikovsky's "Dance of the Reed Pipes."

"In the ballet the instruments actually come to life," explained Billy.

"See if you can put more life into your own playing," said Duke, handing a toy pipe to each saxophone player.

"What am I supposed to do with this?" asked Paul.

"Play it," Billy answered, chuckling. "Duke and I call this movement 'Toot Toot Tootie Toot.' We added a little New York flavor here. Imagine you're an old calliope, pumping out tunes on the Coney Island pier."

With every entrance of the toy pipes, the band broke into giggles.

Duke took over the rehearsal. "Okay, cats. No more foolin' around." He turned to the trumpet players. "You're my Peanut Brittle Brigade. Give me a big fanfare at the opening. Jimmy and I will take over on clarinet and piano."

The band was transported back forty years to the Cotton Club in New York, the birthplace of Harlem jazz. The musicians began to realize what Duke and Billy were doing. Their *Nutcracker* was a melting pot of musical styles past and present.

A Hollywood movie studio inspired the next piece. "We've given the sugarplum fairy a new identity," said Duke. "She's a West Indian beauty now—a starlet of the silver screen named Sugar Rum Cherry."

Billy walked over to the drummer. "Start us off, Sam. Show us how Cherry swings her hips." Sam began playing a hypnotic rhythm.

Billy turned to one of the oldest members of the band and said, "Now it's your turn, Harry. Let's hear Cherry sing." Harry picked up his baritone saxophone and played a sultry tune.

Duke swayed to the music. "That's it!" he cried. Right before his eyes, Cherry strolled through a cane field on a hot, moonlit night.

Just then a tall, gangly man burst into the studio and shouted, "Why, if it ain't my old pals Duke-a-rooty and Strays-a-vouty! The hippest cats of jazz-a-tooty."

Duke gave the visitor a big bear hug. "How's it swingin', Slim?"

"It's swingin' real fine," answered Slim. "I'm cuttin' a new record in the studio down the hall. Old Slim Gaillard is finally making his comeback! Hop-a-tooty and slim-slam-a-booty. Catch you later, cats."

He closed the door behind him and disappeared down the hall.

"That Slim is something else," said Duke. "Let's dedicate our version of Tchaikovsky's 'Russian Dance' to him."

"Great idea," said Billy. "Okay, cats, you're on a steamboat floating down a river."

"Which river?" asked Juan, holding his trombone.

"Good question," said Duke. "Hey, Strays, name a big river in Russia."

"The Volga," said Billy.

"Don't you mean the 'Volga-*vouty*'?" replied Juan.

"We're off to China now," said Duke. "Only in my version we're strolling along Gin Ling Way in Chinatown in Los Angeles."

Billy gave instructions. "Paul and Jimmy, you take the first solos on saxophone."

"Then make way for me on the piano," added Duke.

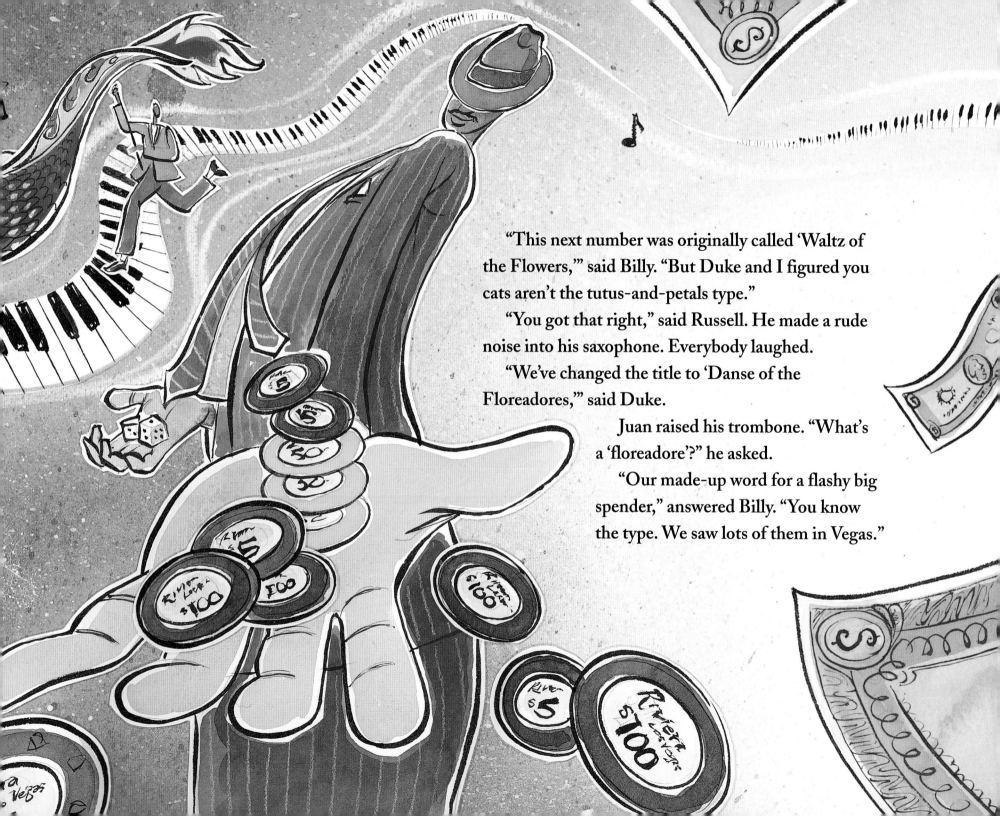

"This next number was originally called 'Waltz of the Flowers,'" said Billy. "But Duke and I figured you cats aren't the tutus-and-petals type."

"You got that right," said Russell. He made a rude noise into his saxophone. Everybody laughed.

"We've changed the title to 'Danse of the Floreadores,'" said Duke.

Juan raised his trombone. "What's a 'floreadore'?" he asked.

"Our made-up word for a flashy big spender," answered Billy. "You know the type. We saw lots of them in Vegas."

The final number in Duke and Billy's *Nutcracker Suite* was called "Arabesque Cookie." Russell started out on a bamboo whistle. Juan kept the beat with a tambourine.

"This movement was inspired by the *Nutcracker* ballet I saw on TV last Christmas," said Billy. "Imagine a tall, stately dancer dressed like a sheikh. Multicolored parrots surround him. Green palm fronds fan his tent. You're in an Arabian oasis."

As the final notes of the *Nutcracker* drifted into the air, Irving burst through the studio door. "Duke, that was fantastic! I heard the whole thing from the sound booth. Your brush with the classics is genius!"

"You sure showed us a thing or two," said Booty. The rest of the band nodded and cheered.

"It wasn't just me," said Duke. "That cat Tchaikovsky was it! And anyway," he continued, putting a hand on Billy's shoulder, "this music is as much Strays's as it is mine."

"I'd like to think our music is beyond category," said Billy, winking at Duke.

"Beyond category, indeed," said Duke.

AUTHOR'S NOTE

This book is based on historical fact. The characters—Duke Ellington, Billy Strayhorn, Irving Townsend, Slim Gaillard, and all the band members—really did exist. Their interactions with each other are confirmed through letters, memoirs, recordings, photographs, film footage, and newspaper articles. The most reliable description of the origins of the Ellington/Strayhorn *Nutcracker Suite* is found in David Hajdu's book *Lush Life: A Biography of Billy Strayhorn* (North Point Press, 1996). Unfortunately, a detailed description of the recording session, which occurred over not one but three days (May 21, May 26, and June 3, 1960), is not available. Consequently I relied on my imagination to fill in some gaps. The titles of the various movements and the album's original liner notes provided valuable information about the inspiration behind the music.

Ellington and Strayhorn composed their *Nutcracker Suite* in less than three months. Close study of the handwritten manuscripts, now housed in the Smithsonian, reveals the importance of Strayhorn's contributions. Strayhorn was a classically trained musician who encouraged Ellington to think outside the box.

Ellington deeply valued the musical personality of each band member, and he always kept in mind a player's unique sound when composing music. I tried to capture this working relationship in the book. The musicians performing on the *Nutcracker Suite* recording are: Harry Carney, Paul Gonsalves, Johnny Hodges, and Russell Procope (saxophones); Jimmy Hamilton (saxophone and clarinet); Willie Cook, Andres Meringuito, Eddie Mullins, and Ray Nance (trumpets); Lawrence Brown, Juan Tizol, Booty Wood, and Britt Woodman (trombones); Sam Woodyard (drums); Aaron Bell (bass); and Duke Ellington (piano).